I only have beautiful experiences
by Gary Bate

I only have beautiful experiences

ISBN 9781838197179
Published September 2022

Blue Light Publishing

Contents

Introduction

You may be sitting upon a chair or a sofa or in bed, reading this book, but what is that? It's an experience.

What have you done in life that's not been an experience of some kind?

Life is an experience and it's full of experiences for us to experience and capture any wisdom therefrom.

We are the sum total of our experiences and what we've captured as wisdom shapes our behaviours.

So experience is very important and what I've just said is the reason we are all here.

We can only be correctly defined by our behaviour and this is shaped by our wisdom, which is reliant on our experiences and what philosophy we've been exposed to.

In that context, this book can be regarded as relevant philosophy; relevant because as you will soon find out - I am talking about life and the nature of this reality.

I will write this in my usual punchy style as I've always preferred to get straight to the point rather than beat around the bush.

So it will be another 'quick read', yet you will probably go back over it to ponder and contemplate the depths of my mind. I hope I've managed to expand you in a conscious way and that you don't regret making the purchase. I can assure you, my intent is pure...

Your Soul is a wisdom hunter and it won't rest until its bag is full! So it nudges you for new experiences and it tries to steer you away from repetitive, addictive experiences. It has a very tough job because it's fighting against your mind parasites that are quick on the uptake.

All thoughts have form and we all have our demons. It's a tug-of-war and we're the rope!

I thought I'd said all I wanted to say after publishing my last book (Pure Mind), but no, there's always more and my work became more succinct. The realisations kept coming and I was often sitting at my machine with the first coffee of the day.

What follows this intro is a selection of those writings, which will seem unrelated to one another; but by the end you'll realise they are pieces of a puzzle that forms a higher conscious point of view in its entirety.

It is not my aim to get people to think like me for I am not an arrogant person. My aim is to encourage you to think for yourself, outside of this mind-controlled society.

If you find my words confrontational or intimidating; that's good! Sometimes we need to be pushed to new facets of us, so we can arrive at greater truths in due course. My quest is to be a free thinker ~ Gary Bate.

We

I want to start by giving you something very deep yet very simple. You may want to re-read this chapter once you've finished the book.

We all have FORM – a permanent form and a detachable form... (all thoughts have form).

Our permanent form is our Spirit and our detachable forms are the bodies we sport in each lifetime.

We always address our permanent form in what we say and how we think and our detachable form simply listens and complies.

It's a fact that we tell ourselves a lot of lies. For instance, our permanent form never gets sick – so any health-related statement other than 'I am radiantly healthy' is a lie!

The truth is making the shift from thinking of yourself as a body to realising you are not your body.

Evolution is progressively ever-deepening personal realisation. It doesn't get any deeper and any more simple than this. Greatness now beseeches you..

Superconsciousness is nothing more than always being conscious of what I've just written. Like me, you will slide off this truth and your body will be affected as a result of you slipping away...

Your detachable form is constantly being affected by

how you think and in particular the conclusions of your thought processes (what you say). Consciousness is everything...

A masterful being only ever addresses (with the truth) what's permanent in him or her. Becoming that masterful being is calling out (naming) the lies as your past-embedded mind gives them to you. You then conclude with the loftiest of truth that applies to your permanent nature.

So, if your body is currently sick, it is actually true to say 'I am radiantly healthy'. This shift is a massive one and this is radical truth that you will never here from anyone else.

If you succeed at 'living your (this) truth', your detachable form will stay attached to your Spirit...

Your body is like a BMW K1300GT (my bike) and you are the rider of it :). Your Soul is like my tank bag that only stays with your biological machine for as long as it works... Your Spirit is like the wind through your hair (helmet!).

Evolution is the upward journey (moving up your kundalini energy) through your seven chakras.

Very few get to the 5th chakra (at the thyroid gland) and only the most pure mind (this is why I wrote the book – Pure Mind) can go beyond that.

You are 'advanced' if you get to the 5th chakra, but be aware – everyone who gets there, gets stuck there!

Why is this? The consciousness at the 5th chakra is 'living and speaking your personal truth without duality'. What happens when your truth is the same as mine – that you are not your body; yet you still live as if you are your body? I'll tell you what happens – you get sick and your destiny doesn't look rosey unless you come back into line with 'living and speaking your personal truth'...

I am currently moving back into alignment and I am a work in progress, like all of you.

You cannot know this truth and live like other people, for if you do, you will fracture at the 5th and manifest some kind of effect in your body. Other people can live out their mind-controlled lives without fracturing at the 5th, because they're not at the 5th – they languor below their waistlines...

If you don't understand this (and you want to) then you'll need to read all of my other books...

I could say a lot more here but I'd only be repeating myself. We are all challenged by the knowledge I have given you here.

Your World Biking Tour is to bring your detachable vehicle (your body) into complete alignment with the Wind (your Spirit). You do that through your mind.

Looking outside of yourself at other people and or the dire state of our World, is nothing more than distraction away from the real reason we are all here. The answer is never outside of us.

I am (you are) consciousness (energy) and my (your) Spirit was the first manifestation of that primal energy (consciousness).

So if we're looking for the correct, permanent identity, Spirit is it!!

Due to our collective, relative, unconsciousness; we have incorrectly identified with our bodies. We all need to reunite with the truth. The aforementioned 'massive shift' is to always be conscious of what our permanent identity is and moreover, to live in accordance with our true identity.

I am Spirit; I am not my Body. I am Healed for I now know the Truth - that I have always been Radiantly Healthy. My body has certainly suffered over the years, but that has been because I acted as if I was it.

Talk can be cheap and these are lofty words. Just affirming your new truth won't cut it. You have to live as it. The 2 must become 1.

If you say you are a god yet you live and behave like other 'humans' then your house is divided (you are energetically fractured at the 5th chakra).

We have to be what we say we are, because we are only ever truly identified by our behaviour.

The Big Apple of Time

Is Star Trek sci-fi or is it channelled knowledge? Does the answer matter? What matters is the irrefutable law of quantum physics, which says that "all times exist simultaneously in the now moment". So when Picard time travels from the 25th Century back to this timelime, we know that that is possible!

So past and future exist now just like slices (timelines) through a big apple. Science has also proven that parallel universes exist, so is there a reality playing out now where Hitler is winning the war?

Now you might think this is wacky and you'd be correct because quantum mechanics is wacky, but it's also true. All times (timelines) exist in the Big Apple of Time.

So just like I said to a friend the other day – we are timeless beings stuck in time...

Enlightenment involves this understanding because we are truly multi-dimensional beings...

As all times exist now and so whatsoever you say about yourself, here and now, is the truth you give to your reality and to your body. You are the truth-giver unto your reality and your body listens and complies.

I love logic – don't you? There's nothing unreasonable about how things work – quantum fact!

So who wins this war and does it matter? How many

times has it played out before? Is there a timeline without puppet-masters? Of course! Why do you think I'm bothering to write to you?

Every thought counts. Your body listens to them all. Your thinking determines which slice of the apple you're in. Is your thinking reactive (emotional)? Is it creative in terms of what you want?

You are the only truth. Whatsoever you say about yourself is the truth you give to your body. Is this the kind of knowledge the temporary authorities of this World would want you to know? Well, it's scientific and yes it's far advanced to their science!

Let me give you an example. They are excited about their gene therapy and their nanotech because it allows them to change our biology. Of course this can be for our benefit or be detrimental. The recent mass vaccinations are the best example. But here's what is superior knowledge – how you think determines your genetic expression.

Can you talk and walk your way into a different slice (another timeline)? How do you know that you haven't already done that?

When you dream of yourself with other people, whom you know but you don't recognise in this slice; are you dreaming of you actually co-existing in parallel?

It is time for a reset, but not the moronic one touted by the Nazis.

Are you emotional and struggling with your weight or are you perfectly balanced? You decide.

Are you in the process of healing or are you healed? You decide.

Are you trying to keep the wolf from the door or are you wealthy? You decide.

Are you becoming knowledgable or are you wise? You decide.

If I say that I have sold millions of my books – is that the truth? Yes it is – it's my truth as I am the truth-teller unto the reality that beseeches me. The thought always precedes the reality...

The Spiral of Time

Just like the water going down your plughole; time spirals down through the energetic dimensions from its fastest time to this slowest time. Your body is a product of this slow time, but your thoughts are much faster. Mass is coagulated thought – thought that has been slowed down through the spiral of time.

When you look in the mirror you are looking at the past because you are looking at what was previously created (cellular change is occuring all the time).

So if you look at your body and acknowledge how it feels, then you are projecting your past into your future. You're wise when you intercede in the process by sending new messages to your body.

I am radiantly healthy (and my body is catching up through the spiral of time and in accordance with how I am behaving). I can only BE what I AM when I behave in unison with what I say I AM.

If we look at reality and re-confirm it, we are projecting it into the future. We have to change the signals we are sending out. Mastery is looking at reality, ignoring it and creating our own.

You cannot do this if you doubt it because your doubt will carve away at your lofty thinking.

*What manifests is your **common** thinking. If you can change the programmes you can change your life...*

What does change and the spiral of time feel like?

Lethargy accompanied by heavy, non-sensical dreams. This is the way your energy comes back to you and that's required for radiant health.

So it's not "I am in the process of healing" it's "I am healed". It's not "I am working on my prosperity" it's "I am fabulously wealthy!"

Please don't send mixed messages that confuse your body - get your head straight on this...

The illusion of time is that it's linear; it's actually dimensional and relates to energetic frequency. All exists in time because time is a condition of energy and all is the manifestation of energy.

If thought (energy) is not the creative ingredient then what is?

Every emotion is an internal state and Joy is no exception to this. What triggers emotions in your life, will not trigger joy. Joy is the emotion of radiant health. Joy is the result of you knowing the truth and engaging it in your life.

Imagine it – radiant health! Truly – imagine it! Talk yourself into it! How else are you going to do it? Your army of cells is waiting for you to wake up and lead it to victory!

I am radiantly healthy. Are you?

I have exactly the correct amount of blood in my body.

My blood pressure is optimal.

My blood viscosity is optimal.

My vascular system is clear of debris.

My heart is strong and beats to perfection.

My eyesight is perfect – I have perfect vision.

I will only wear glasses for as long as it takes for my body to catch up with my truth.

My Body is in homeostasis; it is perfectly balanced.

My Soul is complete; it balances with a feather.

My Spirit is rejoicing as I have achieved what I came here to do, which was to evolve myself.

Is this a help to you? Are you getting the idea? Talk yourself into being the greatest you can be.

Fallen Angels

There are angels who have never lived amongst us. They chose not to descend and they have only ever known love in its purest sense. Are they greater than us? No. We have been them and we chose to continue the journey, to turn love inside out and increase our understanding of it.

Love is the whole orange. Each segment is 'fractured love' (all of the emotions).

When you are being angry, are you being loving? Of course not. Is love real and anger unreal? It's ALL real because what is real is your experience and how you react to it.

We are the fallen angels. We deliberately fell to experience these bodies and this Last Kingdom.

How do I know that you and I are fallen angels? Because we're here...

All of us are experiencing what is not love (emotions) for the purpose of putting the chocolate orange back together again. The trouble is, 99.99% of people have become utterly lost in it all...

Now the game here is power & control. It's the same game in the microcosm (you're relationships) and in the macrocosm where the Firm sits at the apex of the secular power pyramid.

Is there one entity controlling this World? Absolutely!

He's heavily invested in certain emotions...

Are there fallen angels in the Light? Yes. Like us, they fell from LOVE but they never incarnated into these physical bodies. Our sustenance is food and their sustenance is our memories, which is a substitute for the fact they can't experience what we can, by virtue of not having physical bodies.

Those of us who are consciously 'aware', are working at moving back to unconditional love, which is beyond the Light. This is all about mastering our emotional bodies, which is all about gaining in wisdom. It's a very 'personal' journey for each and every one of us.

Can we love 'in spite of'?

You can know something but you can know it even better if you take it apart and put it back together again. We are the brave ones who went inside of love.

Wisdom is key and you will glean much of it by reading my books...

So please relax – no matter how hard you try – you cannot hurry wisdom. Simply desire new experiences and let life teach you. "Beloved God, open me up to know", is a great desire to voice every day.

What is real for us is what we perceive and feel through the senses of our bodies. We are the sum total of our experiences and the wisdom we've gleaned therefrom.

Watch (like a hawk) your ulterior motives for they are subtle aspects of control, which is not love.

Try to treat everyone in the manner you would want them to treat you. This is a live exercise...

Your body is the resemblance of your consciousness – it shows you your state of mind. When you evolve, it heals. Self-love is thus the answer.

Loving it all is understanding it all and accepting the way it is. I don't hate the Firm for wanting to enslave humanity; I understand the aphrodisiac of power and the total lack of a conscience.

When you understand the very personal nature of everyone's Spiritual journey, including your own; you will more easily detach emotionally from everyone.

I write to hopefully help you to find some of your missing pieces...

Freedom

*What is it? To come and go as you please? To be free
of people making demands on you? To be free of your
own addictions? To travel wherever you want to go
whenever you want to go there? To be able to leave
possessions and responsibilities for undefined periods
of time? To be able to experience your every desire?
I'd say it's all of these things, wouldn't you?*

Do we, do you, do I really want to be free?

*Imagine that you can just sit in your armchair, close
your eyes and instantly transport yourself to
anywhere on this planet. No costs of travel, nobody's
permission to get, no I.D.'s to show and no paperwork
to fill in! Would that not be freedom?*

*Further, imagine you could willfully transport
yourself to a parallel universe or to a higher
dimensional frequency, which exists in a different
time flow. Would you go there or would that put
the fear of God in you? I mean, what if you went into
a faster time and when you came back, everyone you
knew were long dead?*

Be logical – consciousness is everything.

*Being a Time-traveller is the only real freedom, but
most people will not desire real freedom because of
their emotional attachments. You can't time-travel if
you are emotional.*

To disappear and re-appear at will in any time-flow,

one has to be free of all attachments – free of all people, places, animals and things...

So it is, upon this planet, the inhabitants do not want to be free and that's why they're not free - consciousness is everything.

The irony is – the very things that enslave us are the very things that we can't take with us. We spend our lives trying to build a false sense of security and we live in the hope that we don't blow it all too early. We do as we're told to do, we comply with any voices of 'authority' and we pay for their permission to travel, which is our God-given birth-right!

We are the authors of our own demise.

Time-travellers have been caught in photographs – they do exist! Just like Star Trek, some come back to try and change something to improve the future.

Do you like to travel? This should be your ideal. You can sunbathe under a golden sun and under a blue sun in the next moment...

Do we need houses? They're just short-term experiences.

Do we need fast cars and bikes? They're just short-term experiences.

Do we need pensions? Yes until we learn how to time-travel.

Do we need animals? They're beautiful, short-term experiences.

Do we need families? Yes until we learn how to time-travel.

Do we need lovers and partners? They're usually just short-term experiences.

Do we really need anything? Yes, we all need to learn how to time-travel and that's all about shifting gears and letting go of all the other stuff we think we need.

Shortly, two-thirds of people will find themselves in survival mode. I've already been there and it helped me to realise the folly of this mind-controlled existence.

We are gallactic time-travellers. How did you think we got here? We lowered our frequency into a human body - that's how. How is it we exist when our body's die? Because we access one of our other bodies in a higher energy frequency - that's how.

Red or Blue Pill

Mastership infers the idea of complete freedom, because how can tyrants control a person who can Time-travel? We are time-travellers but the mastership is achieving that in these 'physical' bodies...

Why bother? It's a good question. The construct of people's lives is the emotional attachment to other people and the need to be relevant in the lives of other people. If a person becomes detached and irrelevant to others, they achieve mastership: but what kind of life do they then have?

It seems we have to completely detach to be completely free, yet we can still have drama and a sense of freedom even when we comply with the draconian laws of the World's tyrants.

We always exist – I have no doubt about that. How we live is up to us. We should never criticise others with our judgmental minds. Everyone is a continuum – let them live how they want to live...

The scientists are still struggling to understand the nature of consciousness because they think in 'physical' terms and thus they think it must be the product of 'brains'. They are so wrong. We are literally swimming in consciousness and our brains receive it and compute it. Our brains are receivers and bio-computers.

The quality of what we receive depends upon what we

are already bogged down with or if we are bogged down at all. It is we who keep firing the same stuff.

Higher chakra thoughts get blocked by a person's attitude, which of course has come from somewhere in their past. Like I said the other day, "When your future becomes more important to you than your past, then you're healing".

So is there a good case for self-mastery or is it better to live to the social norms of everyone else?

Self-mastery means detachment, irrelevance and ostracism. But it also means we get to experience what we've never experienced before. Do we (you) want to go there? Or do you want to live out your time experiencing more of what you've already experienced?

Your Soul has an agenda for your life. You cannot advance your Soul through repetition. If you are 'body-conscious' (like the scientists) you will go for more of the same. Addiction can be very subtle.

What's left 'unfinished' in your Soul becomes the basis of your next life and your next life will be here because you don't know about elsewhere. The problem with that is this World is becoming more and more controlled by the day – so in the future, even a sense of freedom won't exist.

Here and now is where it's at and the best time to become more conscious.

Family is seemingly important to most people, but in the greater scheme of things it's not important. People are emotionally bound and relevant to their families; yet the family genetics is what your Soul is here to own as Wisdom! Do you live for your body and its addictions or do you live for your Soul?

1. We have to know that we are time-travellers.
2. We have to accept that it's our journey to time-travel with our existing bodies.
3. We have to look forward to what we have yet to experience and be excited about that.
4. We have to be patient whilst all our energy comes home through the dream state.
5. We have to understand and accept that we will be lethargic as our energy comes home.
6. We have to know that the price of 'letting go' is to become sovereign and respectful.
7. We have to have faith that there's something better than this humdrum mediocracy served up to us by psychopathic tyrants.

Death

I am somewhat hesitant to write this, but having had many OBE's, I am confident in sharing this very important knowledge and especially so as other knowledge on the subject is scant.

Human conditioning tells us that there are certain things that we cannot know and that we should just trust in the process of death and take pot luck with our desiny. I don't agree with that.

Human conditioning also tells us that 'we all die' and whether or not that's true, it places a great importance on this insight I am about to share.

Where has my knowledge come from? The same place as yours! We learn for others – face to face and reading books (watching videos). We learn from our own experiences and intuitive insights...

So if you feel so inclined, indulge me whilst I share what I know about death:

Firstly, do we all die? It would appear so, but appearances can be deceptive! Do some disappear? Would you get to know of they did? A safer stance is – do we all die?

One thing is for sure – if you plan on dying then you will definitely die because that is the quantum law of the universe. So this is for those of you who plan on dying...(the 99.9999%).

You are you and you always exist in some form. When you first 'pop out' (die) you will be in your Light body and you will be in the frequency that is sandwiched between this frequency and the Light, which is Infrared (the same place that my OBE's occured). You now have 3 options:

Option 1: *keep your back to the Light and stay where you are (in other words - be a ghost). This is a good option if you want to wait for your loved ones to die and join you. Time is faster there and thus the wait is less. You will see others in their Light bodies and you will witness the ugliness of addiction, which is another reason some are there. Emotions keep people there for various lengths of time. You can travel as fast as you can think it and infrared can be very beautiful (cf. Infrared planetary pictures).*

Option 2: *When the Light beckons you, you go to it. The question is – why does it masquerade as love and beckon you? Many have talked about the Light review and what they think happens there to incoming souls.*

It has a purpose and that is to show you your life and in particular what unresolved emotions you have. You're not shown what you've resolved into wisdom.

It all sounds lovely, but in order to show you that, the Light literally strips you of all your memories and replays them to you. In other words – you lose your memories and they go to feed the so-called Lords of the Light, who are best described as energy vampires.

So how are you after that? You're still in your Light

body with a Light body brain and an intact Soul, but no memory of anything – can you imagine how frightening that is? And now you're in a place where everything is exaggerated – good and evil to the extremes! Is it any wonder most plan (Soul plan) to return here, in the hope of completing what is incomplete in them?

This World, Infrared and the Light, all comprise a recycling factory of sorts. Babies are born here with no prior memories – a clean slate with a Soul agenda.

As above so below. As below so above.

Option 3*: Keep your back to the Light and head for the Darkness and the faint light in the distance.*

Has it never occurred to you that you're been lied to about the darkness?

This is you moving consciously beyond the Light – a very smart move indeed! What's in those finer frequencies beyond the Light? What exists where the Gold environment (X-Ray frequency) meets the Blue environment (UV frequency)? Go and find out!

You Soul still seeks completion and you will always need a fleshy body for that; but it doesn't have to be the humanoid body found here and you don't have to lose any of your precious memories with this option.

I hope I have served you and you are now suitably armed for your future.

Spirit

Become aware. Become very aware of your Spirit. Your Spirit is what gives you definition. Without it you are undefined. Your body doesn't define you; it's just your vehicle – lifetime after lifetime...

We have all been hoodwinked from the earliest age. We were incorrectly taught to identify with our bodies.

Living to satisfy the perception of bodily need became the order of the day. The ship was afloat but no-one was at the helm. Never mind, it was all necessary and it's all history/herstory now.

You think you need this pill and that pill but you just need to take your power back by becoming the captain of your ship.

If you address the Lord God of your Being, you are addressing the total of your accumulations – Spirit, Soul and Body. Your Body is your Ship. Your Soul is its First Officer and your Spirit is the Captain. You are the Water it sails on and the Wind it sails through...

A ship doesn't reach its destination unless it has a captain. The captain and its first officer are waiting for you to tell them to take control of your body, which means you have to let go of all of your silly perceptions and let 'those who know best' take control.

We live in an intelligent universe and our bodies are no exception. The proof of what we are can only be discovered by us becoming super-conscious and observing that effect upon our own bodies.

You are the truth and your body bears testament to that. I said in one of my books that the highest consciousness and radiant health are the same thing and I stand by that. You get the latter by shifting from the dense effect of your body to the sublime cause of what defines you through all the ages.

Of course I only write for entertainment purposes so take this with a pinch of salt if you like. It's your prerogative to think your perceptions are greater than what I am writing here.

Your body has the memory of everything it has ever consumed. So if you think you need to pop a vitamin C pill everyday, tell your body to remember what it needs and to create it!

Become the Captain and consciously communicate with your body – it will love you for it!

The 'errors' in your consciousness (where you stray from love) are what find their way into your body. Your body shows you your state of mind and this becomes more evident with your time in it.

There is no mystery to why people get sick – nobody is at the helm!

It's all consciousness, so it's just a matter of how much you get to 'realise'. The only thing that cuts it is if you stand aside altogether – you have to go cold turkey with this...

You have body, soul and spirit. If you let your body run the show then your destiny is death.

Soul simply takes instructions and keeps a permanent record. Soul is caught between the devil and the deep blue sea (your Mind and the Captain).

There is no fight when you do the aforementioned shift. Then the ship sails unhindered to its final destination...

Everyone's got an opinion but very few know this truth. Because of that they're all going to die.

Energy comes home through the dreamstate when you shift up the chakra gears. You're going to sweat it out. It's how you purify. You've done the outward journey; now it's no time to do the return journey.

As always, I hope this helps you with your life.

Christ-like Destiny

Was Jesus (Yeshua) born a Christ or did he become one?

Was Buddha born a Christ or did he become one?

Was Appollonius of Tyana born a Christ...?

If you believe that these great beings were born Christs then you will never entertain the idea that you could become one.

Likewise, if you believe that these entities are Sons of God and God's only Son(s) then you will never entertain the idea that you are also a Son (Daughter) of God.

We've been lied to by perverse men for their own gain. It's time to use pure reason...

Many people (the majority) find out the truth when they pass this World, but then it's too late for them to do anything about it.

If you develop a mind like Yeshua had (has) then you would be Christ-like. How then could you be distinguished from him? Maybe your body looks different to his eh?!

Anyone who becomes Christ-like has clearly attained Christ consciousness. The idea that God only had one or a handful of sons and the rest of us are all bastards of the universe, is just plain ridiculous!

We are all the Sons and Daughters of God and our ultimate personal development is a Christ-like mind – Christ consciousness. That is always the choice for us.

By contrast, Human consciousness is Body consciousness – falsely identifying yourself with your own body. Even saying, "I am a man or I am a woman" is not the truth – it's just an experience you are having...

It was my interest in Self Development that took me deeper and deeper into Spiritual realms. The result?

We are here to move beyond Body consciousness. We are not here to die then find this out and realise we have to come back for another go!

Said another way, we are here to complete our Souls as Soul completion is Christ consciousness.

The Masters spoke Truth when they said that it is easier for a camel to pass through the eye of a needle than a rich man.

Rich people can't give it up for the truth. They are too intoxicated by their wealth and raw power. They can't reason what it must be like to have authentic power.

The question is – can you? Can you give it all up for the truth?

What am I really talking about here? I'm talking about bodies – our addicted bodies. Bodies that are addicted to their own chemicals via the minds of their occupants. Addicted to emotions. Addicted to food. Addicted to sex. Addicted to images. Addicted to how you look. Need I go on?

We have all become addicted to our own bodies (that which we are not!)...

So yeah, enjoy your life. Care about how you look. Gorge yourself on fine food. Romp in the hay! And react emotionally as often as you can. But remember, these are the actions of camels who are going to age and die none the wiser.

The World is but a playground for you to wake up from. I am very awake and I fully intend to go through the eye of the needle.

As for your destiny - you of course have one! But it's not something that's pre-ordained by some kind of mysterious being. It's either the default one or it's the one you set for yourself – you now get to choose your destiny because you are now more aware.

I have a destiny. It manifests as a Time-traveller. It's the only destiny I have. Nothing else matters.

Be clear about your future. Please don't be a victim. Other people have their own destiny and that's very unlikely to coincide with yours. Live your own truth... Ride your own bike...

Whilst the World is distracted to focus on things they think are important; we keep a single-pointed focus on our destiny.

Energy flows where focus goes...

There are higher-conscious, more loving Worlds waiting for our divine presence. The consciousness in this World is crippled from the Top down. We never want to go to the Light because this World is but a mirror of it. We want to go beyond it and to do that, we have to become the Time-traveller.

So destiny is really important and your destiny is only in the hands of a psychic if you put it there.

What about your dreams, which come from your subconscious mind? Do you accept them all? No, you correct them with your conscious mind!

Please remember, super-consciousness is making conscious your subconscious mind. Accept the dreams that line up with your chosen destiny and dismiss the rest of the rubbish!

You're a Divine Awakening Being and I just give you the best clues...

It's your life – navigate it the best you can and set your own destiny. Energy flows where focus goes...

If you follow a guru, you'll die like the guru and get the default destiny, which is the Light trap.

Any kind of devotional service is a trap (an old program). It's time for everyone to wake up...

Evolution

I'm proud to say that I have changed. It was very important for me. It's my evolving evolution...

When I was a young man, sex was the most important thing to me. Now it means nothing to me.

When I was a young man, I was told that there are only 2 certainties in life – death and taxes. The super-rich don't pay taxes and death is optional.

When I was a young man, I thought that my thoughts were private and that reality was something independent of me – that I played in without any consequencies. I learned that it's the opposite.

My thoughts are seen; just as if they are written across the sky. If I think I am going to die then it's 100% guaranteed that I will. Every thought counts in the light of all eternity.

I have lost the fear because I know I am eternal and I only write to help you.

I have no problem with the fact that everyone in my life is in it temporarily. I allow them all to express howsoever they want, for that is my love for them and I would be a tyrant otherwise.

My love for my dogs has taught me a valuable Soul lesson – Responsibility.

I implore you to get in sync with your own Spirit and

Soul and cease being led around unconsciously by your addicted personality.

The Davos crowd are currently collaborating and plotting their next moves to further empower themselves by imposing their collective ideal on all of us commoners. They are the masters of this World and what they say happens. Shortly the WHO will dictate global health policy and doctors will simply administer vaccines (gene therapy) for everyone and for pretty much everything.

Transhumanism is their ideal and their robots will deal with all dissent.

As the global net tightens for those who are lost in their addicted personalities, the conscious choice to become 'Soul-inspired' is critical for one's evolution and future. Now is the time to change gears...

You are an eternal being – you have endless time to your endless life. You can become whatever you want to become. A Human being was just a temporary 'born into' identity you were given.

If you don't wake up to the truth, you will die and be re-born to the dystopian future that's unfolding here.

Planet Earth is nothing more than a recycling factory for the unawakened. The ideal for you and I is to wake up from it and free ourselves.

Even the Russians talk about the emerging NWO. Why? Because they're part of it and all we're seeing is *infighting to determine who controls what territory.*

Putin was pissed because the US (Biden & Co) had the bio-labs in Ukraine. The genetic-engineering-labs are all around the World.

How can you die if you're a Time-Traveller? You can't because your ability to raise the frequency of your body means you can enter the psychic realm or the 'light' whenever you want to. You have the mind to do that. The problem is, you're focussed elsewhere.

Energy goes where focus goes...

The Time-traveller is in your so-called junk DNA. It's not junk; it's your unlimited potential. To be the Time-traveller you have to develop the mind of the Time-traveller – think about it!

As you do (think about it), your energy will slowly come home as you dream and you will feel lethargic as this healing occurs.

It's your life. It's your future. Everyone in your life is transient. Enjoy them and then move onto your next transient adventure. Let go, allow, love and be more free than any bird. That's my suggestion :)

Phantoms

Humanity focusses upon achieving 'Worldly desires' and that is natural to the human mind.

Quantum physics tells us that energy (reality) flows from where your focus goes...

So what happens when your focus moves away from 'Worldly desires' and you turn 'within'?

Your focus and energy will turn to self-mastery...

There is the fantasy life and there is the real life. There is the phantom life of pursuing 'Worldly desires' and there is the 'imageless' real life achieved through self-mastery. It's always your choice.

How we spin everyday situations is divorced from reality because we are overlaying our biases and judgment upon them. The 'thought about' and 'talked about' situations are tainted and distorted by our own emotionally-based attitudes. This 'overlaying' of our minds upon reality is what fantasy is.

True objective observation is the absence of this spin. This is acheived through self-mastery. It's a complete, impartial stance towards all life.

What are emotions? Fantasy – they are the Phantoms at work.

What is masturbation? Fantasy – it's energetically feeding the Phantoms.

What percentage of sex and or love-making occurs between just 2 people? What's in the field?

Self-mastery is not only mastery over this World (This Last Kingdom); it's mastery over the Psychic World (the netherworld) and the phantasms in the Light.

So my friends, we don't want to go to the Light; we want mastery over it and here is where we do it.

The more we live in our minds the more we are in cloud cuckoo land. The journey is to observe without the bias of our own attitudes and judgments – to be absolutely present with life.

We already have a prevalence of VR here without the likes of Meta taking people even further from the truth!

Fantasy is the last mastery on the route to real freedom.

People are quick to criticise, but like the master said, "don't look for the sty in my eye before you've pulled the log out of your own!"

Leave people to make their own mistakes because that's how they learn. Interferring in the lives of others is the lower consciousness of control at work. Let's all go up a gear not down!

We were all born here to live as 'phantoms amongst phantoms' and to become lost in it all. We've achieved that, because we didn't even know what I've just said.

Imageless

Through our evolution (involution) we acquired (accumulated) forms (images), the most gross of which, we have falsely identified with.

Are we the form(s)? Well yes, but we are really the imageless energy that the forms have been created from. We like to see pictures of our grossest form, yet we're not seeing what we really are.

Imagine if everyone was translucent and you could just make out their outline – just enough to hold a conversation with them. That would change everything and allow everyone to evolve very easily.

Think about the fixation we have with the first chakra. That's gone without any images! If we want to own that one and move our energy higher, we simply have to put a stop to all images...

Love is the answer because only with self-love will we become imageless in our attitudes...

This is the evolutionary task we all face, albeit that I am now only just bringing it to light.

We shouldn't fear the fact that we are merely 'energy & consciousness' because everything is a form of energy and thus our bodies are mere accumulations to what we are. We should look after them...

But how far do we want to let our personal realisation go? Can we live in these gross bodies yet be imageless in our minds?

The evolutionary journey is moving one's Kundalini energy from the consciousness of the lower 3 chakras to the consciousness of the the higher 4 chakras (the so-called higher self).

The common aspect of the consciousness of the 3 lower chakras, is image – image consciousness.

Would you love the people in your life if you could only make out their outline? Maybe you'd love them more?!

What we really love is the 'unseen'.

Please scrutinise your life. You'll see that it's image-driven. What are you doing at the behest of other people? You can play the game all the time or you can live the truth.

You're not going to get this from anyone else on the planet. That's not because it's complicated; it's actually very simple. Isn't it a fact that we've all become too complicated?

I promise you – you'll get more from this wee book (in terms of expanding your consciousness) than you'll get from spending your money on gurus and teachers of all descriptions.

I feel like I have put myself in an enviable position, because I can give unconditionally to whoever wants to read my material and it matters not to me whether you decide to invest in any of my books. I continue to post writings to my website for anyone to read.

Spiritual growth, advancement, enlightenment, total self-realisation, ascension, time-travel etc., is all about becoming IMAGELESS in your mind and in your attitudes.

The less I associate with what I see in the mirror, the happier I become.

If we are 'energy & consciousness' in its purest aspect, then what aren't we?

The scientists have now proven that the big bang theory is bullshit and it's just been more lies. We should always question mainstream science, because these are people that try to understand everything from 'physical' perspectives.

My final (7th) book will be a book of my quotes. I will call it something like Quotes about Consciousness, which is the same as Quotes about Life! To understand the nature of reality, the scientists need to start at the spring not the sea!

Manifestation

I've often wondered why (through the spiral of time) my lofty affirmations didn't materialise into my life? Especially so, given the substantial amount of time I've been affirming parrot-fashion!

Finally the coin dropped for me.

What is your deeper self? What is your god within? What is your Spirit – your Holy (wholly) Spirit? It's the OBSERVER in you.

Your 'observer' is non-judgmental, whereas you run what you see through your analytical brain and thus you judge it.

If you could set aside your mind, you would be the pure observer – viewing as the god/spirit.

Our brains cannot distinguish between what we're looking at and what pictures/thoughts we hold in front of our deeper self (the observer).

When we observe our realities we confirm them into being (quantum physics). There is no reality without an observer. It's the observer that is creating reality (collapsing energy and gluing it back together again).

So we create realities based upon our own biases and the judgments we make.

We know that the brain works via association and repetition. So what happens if we change the view of the observer – away from the environment that's already been created (the past manifested) to a conscious intent that we want to create?

In other words, we defy reality and create our own!

So you decide what you want to create and you sketch it, hence you have a permanent reminder; then you focus upon it. You have made the association and by focussing upon it, you have repeated it.

You go for a walk and instead of judging the environment, all you can see in your 'minds eye' is your picture. Now you may also have a statement (in the now tense) that you've associated with your picture. As you walk, you see your picture and you affirm your statement – seeing the words as you say them to yourself...

My past affirmations never worked for me because I was simply playing lip service to them. It has to be done consciously, with intent and sincerity. You are giving it to your god and thus telling your god what you want – be sincere!

If you're not much of an artist or not inclined to put crayon to paper, then choose a symbol or an element of the environment to associate with. For example: when I look upon flowers (trees etc.) I affirm that "I am entirely beautiful and I only have beautiful experiences". Likewise, you could look upon the sun and feel its radiant rays, "I am radiantly healthy and all is well in my World".

Now of course some of you will think this is poppycock but you can only prove me wrong if you engage this sincerely and it doesn't work. Remember, you have to give it time and much repetition...

If we can prove to ourselves that we can defy reality and consciously create our own, then how far can we take that? If we prove it; we become truly free.

Words can by empty or they can be very powerful. It's the intent and sincerity that manifests them.

The third and final stage or phase of self-development (becoming enlightened) is that there is no distinction between the observer in you and the observed (the observer is observing itself).

Can you observe your mind – your thoughts? Yes you can. That means that you are not your mind.

You are the observer but you have clouded the view with your judgmental mind. What are you showing to your god everyday? Is it repetitive? Is your god (spirit & soul) getting bored?

It's all in the observation...

What are you showing to your god? Are you showing a perfect mirror? Or are you showing a judgment, a criticism, an argument, a frustration, anger, other emotions? What are you seeing? Can you look at the same situation yet change the observation (view)?

Unconsciousness is when you just experience without

*being aware of the observer. Self awareness
is just that – being aware of an observer within you.
Enlightenment is when you are the observer,
observing yourself observing (no judgment and no
ulterior motive of trying to be relevant).*

*We have to change our minds in order to change the
observation. We have to understand that what sits
deep within us (the observer) is us!*

God is within us and we are the gods!

*God can only come through us when we move the
'human' consciousness out of the way. That's the
training of the mind and what the Great Work is all
about. It is up to us to close the gap by purging the
dualism in our minds.*

Can you see your hands coming together?

*If I embrace a beautiful flower or a tree or one of our
2 dogs, I can see their beauty; but what I am seeing is
a mere reflection of me. So I hold our dogs and I
affirm the truth, which is, "I am entirely beautiful". In
doing that I am showing that to my god and
recognising the god within me. The 2 become 1.*

*The only thing we have to do to know the truth is to
move the lower personality out of the way...*

*The more I learn (through my own contemplations),
the more I realise that enlightenment is simple. It is
we (us) who have become complex!*

We do what we think is important and that is often for our own self-importance or to make us relevant in someone's life. We revere human behaviour aka emotional intelligence and ignore the fact that there is no intelligence in emotions and we are not human beings; we are gods who are having temporary human experiences.

The 'change-back' is a change in your observation, which equates to a change in your mind.

Whatever you're thinking is what you are forcing your deeper self to observe and this forms the basis of your life. You consciously create when you become super-aware of what you're entertaining in front of your deeper self.

Please be careful about what thoughts you entertain (what you force your observer to view). Be honest with yourself. Why do you do what you do? Are you feeding any images? Are you always showing your true motives? Are you sincere or insincere? Are you acting to be relevant in someone's life? Why?

The importance of this is this – we are all here to evolve (change) ourselves and that is a steady journey towards becoming the perfect mirror for the perfect mirror within. This is what the great master meant when he said, "the Father and I are one" (I am my Father's mind). No gender inferred.

We must become conscious of our observer and know that it is our perfect inner reflection, which we are to match via gradually polishing ourselves. The more pure our thinking becomes the more inline we get with our deeper self. It is always there. It doesn't come to us because we block it. We are to go to it, by moving out of the way that which is not in alignment with it.

It's there, within you, observing. What do you want to show it? The same old repetitive stuff? It's time for a new paradigm. Remember, your observer sees both what you're looking at and what you hold in your mind and therefrom your reality is being created.

Where did I put them crayons?!

Relevance

It's so simple and so subtle that we've overlooked it!

In my other books I've talked about the Spiritual advancement gained through emotional detachment and how we are attached to places, animals and things and more overtly to people.

The idea that we should detach from other people, even our own family, is horrifying to most people – why is that?

There is a fear we all have and it's being irrelevant. Unconsciously, we have been and are motivated by our desire to be relevant in other people's lives. We act in ways to make ourselves relevant. These actions can seem irrational to others because they haven't reasoned why we are acting in such ways.

When we act tyrannical or like a victim – why is that? Because we want to be relevant.

We control others to make ourselves relevant.

We argue to make ourselves relevant.

Addiction is about relevance.

Following, worshipping and or serving others is about you being relevant in their life.

Bending over backwards to try and please others, is about you trying to be relevant.

When someone asks you the question - what do you do? And you feel like you've got to justify your existence in their eyes – that's you trying to be relevant.

Going out of your way to try and be relevant when you're naturally not, is you being insincere.

It's not about wanting to be wanted or wanting to be loved; it about you wanting to be relevant.

I'm labouring this because it's very important yet very subtle. If you can see it at work in your own life, you will also see the opportunity to retire it.

I can see how my need for relevance has motivated my whole life, even the 25 years of writing I've done! My addictions were grounded in me trying to be relevant. My place in other people's lives, was me being relevant to them and they to me. There's nothing wrong or bad about us always trying to be relevant; it's the human way to be relevant.

It's the Spiritual way to be irrelevant.

People need to understand that there's no correlation between Human behaviour and Spiritual behaviour. The latter is beyond and a mastery over the former.

Please don't underestimate what I am saying here. I got the heads up on this from someone else, who I am very gratefull to for this insight. This is as subtle and as simple as it gets!

What do you do?

It's always bugged me when people ask me, what do you do? I know why they ask it but I can't give them the kind of answer they expect.

The truth is, we are all doing the same thing, but only a handful of people know this.

We are like fish in water. We are swimming in the river of consciousness and we are choosing, consciously or unconsciously, what thoughts to entertain us. This shapes our realities.

Simple isn't it?! But how many people know it, understand it, accept it and work with it? Very few.

The unconscious haven't made the connection between their thinking and their life and the doggy state of their health. They think life just happens to them and thus they're always victims.

I had the thought yesterday that I had a cold coming on. How can I be radiantly healthy and have a cold in my head? I can't! Opposing thoughts create an energetically divided house (body).

Your life is constantly forming around the thoughts you entertain and particularly the thoughts you conclude with. So if I self-correct and think/say, I feel like I've got a cold coming on but I am radiantly healthy so I can't have, then I am in sync with the only statement (regarding one's health) that should ever come out of anyone's mouth!

Consciousness is everything and consciousness creates reality. It constantly affects you and it's only you who decide which thoughts you entertain and conclude with. You do it to yourself.

So to answer the question, what do I do? Here is my answer: I work 24/7 at self-mastery.

This book is my final work, with the exception of a quote book I'm working on. The content here is my truth, but I have yet to live 100% true to it. I am working on it. I am a work in progress, just like you.

I have understood why masters say very little. They only entertain the loftiest thinking and they are reluctant to share that with the masses.

Humans are 'social' beings – they choose social consciousness from the never-ending river of consciousness. They like to be liked and to be popular.

There's nothing bad or wrong in that; but it is the propagation of 'limited' realities.

My books are not for the masses who revere Human, Social Consciousness.

Choose what you show your god within (the observer) very carefully. Self-correct when you need to. The river contains all thought (it's unlimited) and you have the free will to choose which ones you shape your life with.

Do make your power statements and always conclude

your thinking with one of them. Make sure they are in the now tense (starting with I or I am). I could say more here but I'd just be repeating what's in my other books...

Your deeper godself is observing what you choose from its river and it always says, "ok if that's what you want". I'd say you now know what super-consciousness is.

We can't get it from a book or from what someone else says because our reality is our experience of it and we are the sum total of our experiences – nothing more and nothing less. The thought precedes the experience, so we can't experience something we're not aligned with in our thinking. For example, we can't experience radiant health unless we think of ourselves as being radiantly healthy. Of course, this also applies to wealth and everything else...

Responsibility

Being responsible is always being able to respond to situations instead of reacting to them. A response can be to do nothing! A response is thoughtful. A reaction comes from an emotional weakness. Thus the more wise and the less emotional we become, the more responsible we become...

If we try to alter the behaviour of others then we are being tyrants. We are being loving when we do not interfere in the lives of others.

"Express how you want to express and allow others the same grace." That's my motto ~ Gary Bate.

I predict 'they're' going to push us to extremes. I expect this war will continue and we will all be faced with not only food shortages, but electricity (gas) and water shortages too. I also think we're not over with Covid (pandemics) and the next pandemic will hit us very soon (because their warnings are coming directly from their plans). To complete this dystopian picture, we know their Central Banks will soon introduce their progammable digital currencies, which they will use to control us; just like they controlled (and robbed) the Canadian truckers for their dissent.

The above paragraph is not fear-mongering; it's being aware of what's coming. Why do you think they're getting rid of civil-service jobs and funding Ukraine to proliferate this war? It's all in the Globalist's (the Davos crowd's) plan.

With the advent of further lockdowns (pandemic & climate), travel restrictions for us non-compliant ones and controls over the availability of our own money and how we can spent it; the ability to navigate to a self-created dream: is becoming more and more difficult by the day...

Our saving grace is to go within and to get to know the truth. I now know why the Great Master said to God everyday, "Beloved God open me up to know". It's because death is the result of not knowing enough and the above desire is what opens up the brain to receive higher consciousness.

Try and be logical; it's more reliable than emotions.

You have a body and you have a Soul and you have a Spirit. Your Spirit controls your Soul and your Soul controls your Body. So who controls your Spirit?

Believe it or not, it's a great question and there's only 2 possible answers!

Either you control your Spirit or it's controlled by some force outside of you. If the latter then we're all victims to that force. If it's you, then it must be a higher-conscious aspect of you – a part of you that you're currently unaware/unconscious of.

Who tells your Spirit to call your Soul out of your Body at the point of Death? Is it you or is your Spirit an entirely different entity to you and a law unto itself? Who's playing who?

Some people think there are things one cannot know – they're the kind of people who don't want to know and just bury their heads in the sand. Who says you can't know all of the important stuff?

The variable in all of this is mind and what you really are – consciousness. If we are not victims and there are higher-conscious aspects of us running the show, then we have a super-conscious journey to make and complete...

Is that not a responsibility?

Climate Change

Some people don't believe in it, but the climate has always changed cyclically. There have been previous periods of heat followed by ice!

So are we witnessing another cyclical change or is it man-made? Neither! It's elite-driven...

Did we ask you for petrol engine vehicles? Did we ask you for plastics? Did we ask you to cut- down the great rain forests? No! You gave us fossil fuels when the hydrogen fuel-cell was available. You suppressed the technology in favour of your own profits. So let's set the record straight:

We are witnessing Elite-driven Climate Change and that is what it should be known as.

We don't need global governance to deal with climate change; we need the elite to clean up their own mess. Equally, we don't need artificial intelligence (robots) to replace the human workforce; which is the goal of the elite. And we don't need a Universal Basic Income; we need the elite to stop fucking about with our lives...

The Elite-driven Climate Change goes beyond fossil fuels and cutting down trees and the use of pesticides etc.. They are engaged in climate change via their geo-engineering operations (the Chemtrails that are obvious in our skies). For more information on this please go to:

https://www.geoengineeringwatch.org/

Are we headed for a 'Day after Tomorrow' scenario? It certainly looks like it. The evidence Dane shares with us all, proves that we're on a collision course and it's all down to the Davos elite.

Global governance isn't the answer to climate change; it's the cause of it. It has been created to usher in their global governance.

Weather warfare is a secret weapon only because the masses are still sleeping. Look the other way and follow the elite-driven mainstream news...

Wherever there's money to be made, they are there. They will bake us and cut our throats! Just remember, Klaus is on video saying that Putin was one of their 'Young Global Leaders', which means Putin is 'one of them'.

My work is the only credible alternative to the algorithmic future being steered by the elite. Why do we need robots that may or may not become sentient beings when we are sentient beings?

Let us not let these crazy elites make us redundant. The idea of complying with what they say in order to get a regular 'basic' handout from them, should horrify us all. It may not be here quite yet, but it's coming as sure as night follows day...

Carbon dioxide is the gas of life; it's what the trees need to give us the life-sustaining oxygen. Carbon is not the enemy! Let us not take the blame for what are not our crimes.

You can't take it with you

I've always said (throughout all of my books) that evolution is the reason we are all here – after all, why else do we have Souls? Our Souls are programmed for evolution! This means we are here to change ourselves from the 'born into' identity into the real identity...

So what does that mean? It means freedom! We do not have freedom in this World; that's an illusion here – we can only go to where they allow us to go...

The abilities to bi-locate and time-travel are the only real freedoms and they correspond with our real identity.

What we strive to achieve, possess and accumulate here; are the very things that bind us to this World and thus prevent us from experiencing real freedom.

To evolve you have to learn the truth about yourself – you have to know what your real identity is and then slowly become it, which means you purge your 'born into' false identity and slowly modify your behaviour to match your real identity.

Your actions (behaviour) have to match what you say you are, otherwise you are divided against yourself. For instance, if you say you are Vulcan but you act like Human then you are Human. It is your behaviour that determines what you are.

Evolution – learn it, speak it then become it.
The truth is – there are no limits to us, but we limit

ourselves because we keep the same focus...

We atrophy and die because we don't evolve – because we don't become more unlimited. We have to somehow shift the focus from the known onto the unknown and make the unknown known to us.

My previous book – Pure Mind – is a real challenge to limited thinking and limited thinkers.

Christ is a Time-Traveller. How can you die when you've mastered time? Enlightenment is all about mastering time. There are 2 chapters about time at the beginning of this book.

We all have the choice – we can continue to focus on the things that limit us or we can dream a new reality into being.

Growth (wisdom) for your Soul isn't always obvious. Sometimes much wisdom can be garnered from pain and suffering and likewise from various forms of disablement. Your Soul thinks nothing of creating a disabled lifetime just to learn one lesson.

The opportunity for you is not to wait for your next lifetime because you might be less conscious next time around; it's to sieze the opportunity now and free yourself from centuries of enslavement.

You can't do it for anyone else and only you can do it for you. I'm just trying to help you.

Wisdom is the Hunter

Do you know how powerful a scientific statement like The Observer affects Reality is? What about the statement – Consciousness is Everything? Do these seemingly unrelated statements mean anything to you in the context of your life? Probably not.

Here's a couple of bits I just got from google:

It has been suggested that the locality of information transfer in quantum entanglement indicates that reality is subjective, meaning that there is an innate inseparability between the physical system and the conscious mind of the observer.
Summary: One of the most bizarre premises of quantum theory, which has long fascinated philosophers and physicists alike, states that by the very act of watching, the observer affects the observed reality.

This is really powerful because it means we can change reality with our minds and a person who does this is called a master. That is what a master is.

If anyone is so stupid to tell you that they are a master, your retort should be – prove it! A real master can always prove it...

Why is this science (quantum physics) so important? Because if one can instantaneously change reality, one is immortal and where do you draw the line?!

Quantum physics says we can change water to wine,

by seeing wine where there's water. So why don't we all do that today? Because we think we've got better things to do...

It clearly takes a very powerful mind to instantly alter reality. Their focus would need to be intense (the ability to see what's not apparently there) and one would need enough personal energy and intent to affect the structure of mass-coagulated consciousness.

We don't do it because we don't have the focus on it and we don't have enough personal energy. We have placed our energy elsewhere – on other people, places, things, work, activities and everything we think is so much more important than self. We have made a habit of giving our power away...

Mastership is firstly taking your power back and most of that is wrapped up emotionally. A master in the making is hunting down his/her energy and bringing it home. The discord you experience between your thinking and your life, is due to your energy being widely dissipated.

*It's not about taking other people's energy; it's about taking back your own. **Wisdom is the Hunter**.*

My motivation in writing is just to make you think more deeply, because when you do so, you expand yourself immeasurably. Here is a piece you may like - it's about the 'miracles' of Yeshua Ben Joseph. I hope it tantalises you as much as it did me – enjoy! https://www.ramtha.com/content/pdf/teachings/yeshua.pdf

Navigate your Life

Do we try to successfully navigate our lives in accordance with our souls or do we just live haphazardly and try to look after our seeds? It depends upon how conscious we are.

On the current trajectory you're going to die – then what? Do you know the answer? If you don't, you've got a looming big problem ahead of you!

I was an ignorant man – totally lost in this illusion. When I first heard that 'Consciousness is Everything', my ears pricked up but that statement had no real immediate impact on me – it just kind of got parked somewhere in the back of my mind. But now it's at the forefront of my mind and I'm suggesting that it should also be at the forefront of your mind – because it's super-real important!

Consciousness is everything. Your every thought is creating your life right now and for all times. If you think you have no other option (you think like a victim) then those are your thoughts that are impacting your life. Everyone can always say NO.

What kind of Government gives away its power and the sovereignty of its people to a privately owned NGO? That's what's happening right now.

Governments are empowering the WHO to legally dictate the policy (the response) for the next pandemic, which is in the pipework...

So tomorrow we're going to get another pandemic and the governments are going to tell us that they have to comply with the WHO, which will impose mandatory vaccinations and lockdowns...

If you think you are free on this planet then you need a good shaking.

The fascist train can no longer be stopped but we can still all say NO.

The fascists do not know what's best for you; they only know what's best for them and that's what they always put in place.

You comply, you die and you comply again because you haven't got a clue what's going on.

Broadly speaking, all consciousness can be split into 7 identifying qualities. It's best to think of these as gears and your body as the vehicle. The first 3 gears are a dual shift (the duality of male and female and all freaks). Being focussed upon survival and or sex keeps one in 1st gear. Being emotional keeps one in 2nd gear and being focussed on power (control over others) keeps one in 3rd gear. The most powerful people on this planet are stuck in 3rd gear and everyone is stuck in one of the first 3 gears, because if they weren't they wouldn't be here!

You will never buy, eat or fuck your way out of your predicament. Your evolutionary journey is purely through the labyrinth of your mind – consciousness is EVERYTHING.

Mastery over your Body

In the end, death or ascension, comes down to mastery over your own body.

I'm talking MASTERY. I'm not saying I'm a master like some ignorant folks say. I'm talking about the reason we're all here and what that comes down to in the end.

You don't have to swim under ice or bungee jump or absail down rock faces to achieve it. Those pursuits are for the 'big images' who happily bolster their images and their bank accounts...

Self-mastery is purely an internal matter and it's something an astute observer does all the time. They challenge and purge their minds of all the dros they've entertained in the past.

The top prize and living in the now means dumping the past and walking free into the future...

We must recognise that minds are built by associaton and repetition, so anything you've lingered on in the past is neurologically embeded in you and your mind will give it back to you if your train of thought has any association with it.

Completely unhinging from the past then is active work for everyone who accepts their journey.

Fantasy isn't necessarily salacious or the stuff of fairy tales; it can be thinking you're going to fall off your bike, when there's no logical reason for that.

When you sharpen up, you'll see that fantasy is rife in you and it's your job to identify it and dismiss it – call it out and get your head straight!

Memory is as frequent a visitor as you let it be. You certainly have a past but you don't have to live there. Forgive it, get the wisdom from it and move on...

So where does your body come into all of this? Touch! Touch invokes both memory and fantasy...

Mastery = no fantasy and no 'lived in' memories.

Forget about the ice man; I'm talking real self-mastery here and the very reason we are all here!

On a cellular level, bodies degenerate due to repetition. For instance, everytime you get angry you are degenerating your body. Every reaction degenerates and every new experience regenerates. It's like inking a stamp. The first few times you use it, they all look pretty much the same. Eventually, the ink runs out and you can't make out the image.

Your cells effectively wear out unless you know the art of rejuvenation and you are living it daily.

Your body and your mind are NOT separate. Only YOU can reign your mind in. I hope I've brought you new meaning to 'going within'; it's not sitting there with your eyes closed and getting someone else to take a picture of you – so that you can put it on FB and tell everyone how enlightened you are :)

It's only wisdom that gets your mind out of the past. Being stuck in time is being stuck in the past. I can only help you by causing you to contemplate.

If you're wise you'll start to unwind and you'll actively purge every day and night. You're not here to play games or to serve others; you're here to master this environment, which includes your body.

Have you got your Map?

Every entity carries a Soul (just like a handbag) and although the Soul has a pre-planned agenda for the new lifetime, it does an exceeding poor job at communicating its intention for completion. It's got the map for the new life but it's like the Sat Nav is switched off!

Souls are blown to smithereens here because instead of following what's been programmed in them, they follow other lost Souls.

So what can you do now that you're in yet another vehicle and your Sat Nav is kaput? Keep driving around in circles?

There is a plan that gets you to the destination but rather than being directed by satellites, it's kind of like a treasure hunt! You follow the plan, you get the treasure and you finally arrive.

The destination is all about the attainment of individual qualities, which become your modus operendi. For instance, one of the qualities is 'giving without any conditions attached'. A condition can be as simple as just wanting other people to think a certain way about you. With this in mind, I have decided to offer free counselling to anyone who needs my help. For me, it's currently the best way I can give to people I've never met. By doing so I claim my treasure...

gary at whatstress dot com

I only have beautiful experiences

The illusion of life is the fantasy; it's what your mind makes up and you live to. Please reign it in...

I'm now going to list the qualities you need to find in yourself in order to arrive at your desitination:

1. Accept your equality with all other beings. Never follow, worship or adore another being because all are your equal. Never see yourself as superior or inferior to anyone. You cannot 'arrive' unless you see yourself as God sees you.

The privileged few on this planet have the same challenge as those with low self-esteem. None of these treasures can be missed in order to 'arrive'.

2. Staying calm and being patient is a big one for all of us. It's not really number 2 here; it's more the culmination of the journey. Clearly there's a lot more detail, but I've already put it in my other books...

3. Being 'ulterior motive free' is one of the essential qualities and treasures. It's all about your smell. The purer your mind becomes the more beautiful the fragrance you emit.

4. No judgment is a golden treasure. We must never forget that nothing would exist if God had judged anything. Unconditional allowance and acceptance of 'how things are' is the same as taking a non-judgmental stance.

5. Forgiveness is an essential treasure. If we cannot forgive someone then we are sitting in judgment upon them and that drains our energy not theirs.

6. Stop the fight with life. Respect other people's choices. If you judge you're a fool.

7. The identity given to you is a facade. You are what underpins it. You are not a Body (a human being). You are not a Soul (thats just a kind of emotional accounting system). You are not even your first form (your Spirit), but it's a massive step forward to identify with your Spirit; because otherwise you are left with the formless energy & consciousness.

Is it time to redefine yourself?

Your Soul is basically useless to you, in so much as it doesn't effectively help you in any way. You have to work it out for yourself and go on your own treasure hunt! I hope I've managed to point you in the right direction. Specific, individual, Soul journeys will include some and maybe all of the above treasures.

There has to be Love

"To me there has to be love and I know that that love can only come from me" – Gary Bate.

So I continue to give unconditionally...

Is there a creative force in your life or does life just happen to you? I guess if I asked that question to 4 random people, 3 would say the latter...

The 'conscious' will say it's both – sometimes I'm creative and other times things just happen. The super-conscious will recognise that they are the core of everything that occurs in their life.

There are just 2 minds you can be in – consciously creative or unconsciously creative. You are creating your life, whether or not, you are aware of it. Let's take a look at both minds:

Unconsciously creative

Essentially, it's a reactive mind that's out of control because the person hasn't woke up to what's going on. Their mind dwells in their past so their future will continue in the same way. Their mind plays 'what if' scenarios and thus they get caught up in creating their scenarios. Their mind often slips into fantasy land and that can be about literally anything; thus their life is living in their mind's fantasy.

Entertainment alleviates dull days. Emotional addiction is rife because emotions are based in the past. Other addictions are also commonplace. This is the optional 'reactive' life.

Consciously creative

They (we) know that every thought counts... It's a matter of only holding in front of the observer the thoughts that are wanted and training the mind (by concluding all thought patterns with wanted thoughts). Super-consciousness is you steering your mind to where you want to go...

When you're super-conscious, you will be razor-sharp (nothing will get past you that's unwanted). You will know that whatsoever you say about yourself is the truth and that you are the truth-giver unto your reality (because quantum physics clearly states that all times exist simultaneously in the now moment).

You also know that if you entertain conflicting thoughts, you will be a divided house on an energetic level. You know that you have an observer who is always 'on' and what you force your observer to view is what you are telling your observer that you want.

Enlightenment is as simple as sorting what you want from the trash. Could it really be that simple? Yes it is. But here's why people do the complex instead of the simple:

The complex is about other people. It's about family and relationships and drama and difficulties and all those feel good feel bad emotions. The simple is not about any of that. It's just about YOU.

Affirming a greater reality than the one that seemingly beseeches you is you being a MASTER.

There is a creative force in your life and it's a never-ending river of thought... What you 'freeze-frame' from the river is what shapes your future life. You are doing it all to yourself.

My work will never be popular because it's not what people want to hear. Growing up in consciousness is about becoming responsible for how you think and what attitudes you have. If I only get to help one person with this book; it's worth my efforts.

The effect of Love

It must be over 26 years since I started to write and I did so because I was estranged from my 2 children and I thought it would be a good way to help them with their lives. Their mothers simply wanted money from me, which unfortunately I didn't have. With very limited access, writing was the way I tried to give them something meaningful and valuable in terms of their souls. Of course, as the years notched up, I realised that I was really writing for everyone, including myself.

Like Mo, you can beat yourself up over your past and most people do that. You can literally crucify yourself over it. You can become riddled with guilt because of it. You can be full of regret and never accept that you had to do what you did to know what you know.

The wise thing to do with your past is to ditch it completely. What does it matter? It doesn't matter. It's irrelevant. Be proud of what you know and understand that you know what you know today because of the EXACT way your life has played out...

It's time to walk away with the wisdom. A new life awaits all of those who are still playing emotions that are based in the past. Let it go – it's not important; it just limits you.

I'm writing this because as I sat drinking my first coffee of the day, I started to have fond memories of my deceased grandparents, which led my mind to think of my siblings (minds work by repetition and ASSOCIATION). My grandparents are now, once again, enjoying life in their thirties...

So you see, I am able to write this for anyone who wants to read it and that is the unconditional beauty of writing. I continue to write short pieces and post them to my website – job done!

As I've said many times before, everyone's journey is very personal and they must find their own way in life. The very best we can do for anyone, is to share wisdom that can unhinge them from their past...

No teacher, no guru, has the answer for you; because unhinging from the past is also unhinging from them! You don't need a teacher or a guru; you just need to understand that the highest possible achievement in life is Christ consciousness and that means NO PAST.

Why do we have a past and get all emotional about it? Because we have insufficient wisdom!

Your teacher and your guru are going to die and so are your parents (if they're not already dead). It's not wise to follow anyone.

Everyone dies right? No. You just don't travel with the time-travellers because you're still stuck in the past.

There's only so many ways I can say this.

So what are the effects of wisdom and enlightenment? Letting go of the past...

You never did anything wrong. You are not accountable to anyone. You are not superior or inferior to anyone. You owe everyone nothing. You hold guilt because it's a feeling and you don't know who you are without feeling good or bad about something!

The prizes and certificates of this World will not save you. The adrenaline-pumping competitve feats that you win will only falsely define you. You are wanted.

A higher, deeper, power, wants you to see through all of this illusion and return with your bag full of treasure (your soul full of pearls of wisdom). That's your real journey. You're not here to serve anyone or live for family. You're here to become the real you.

I'm trying to kick you out of the nest and you're holding on for dear life. It's a beautiful day here – sunny and 21 degress; so I'm now going out for a blast on my new motorbike, then I'll write the final chapter when I return.

Walk as a god

It seems we all learn really slowly but I guess that's just the way it is. We are stubborn creatures and natural 'know it alls' that our own attitudes grossly slow down our learning. If only we had open, uncluttered minds that the highest echelons of consciousness could pervade our entire beings.

I have said that "we are gods" but what does that mean if we don't live as gods? It means nothing!

Could we really be gods in sheeps clothing (garments of limitation) who are living as the garment instead of walking as gods? I believe so...

Is the 'walking as a god' the equivalent to the completion of your Soul? My logic says it is...

We wonder why we struggle to manifest what we want in this life and the reason is quite simple – we don't have enough energy (higher consciousness).

Money is energy for sure and with enough of it, one can buy almost anything. But money won't redeem you or stop you from looking over your shoulder or create for you a fabulous future beyond materialism.

We've been leaking energy since the day our bodies were born. Thinking in duality is what causes the haemorrhaging and we are now 'experts' at that. The primal cause is thinking you're the garment.

Now really I just write for entertainment purposes

because everything I write is meaningless unless it is lived and thus proven.

Can we swim into shore whilst everyone else is swimming out to sea? Can we live as gods whilst wearing human-looking bodies? Can we rise above the limited mindset that comes from garments?

This is the quest. This is the true Spiritual journey. This is the very reason we are all here. Am I the only one who can see this?

A truly Spiritual person is a 'energy hunter'. They hunt down the energy they have unwittingly given away through the course of their life. Their energy is with other people and places and things...

Becoming aware of where your energy is 'caught up', is you moving to a soulfull life. Believe it or not, it's all in your mind; but let's take a look at some common areas where your energy might be caught up:

1. There's someone you can't or won't forgive

2. You're not being honourable

3. You're emotional about someone or something

4. You're being a tyrant or a victim

5. You're in some kind of devotional service to someone or some organisation

6. You're treating others in less than loving ways

7. You're not loving yourself enough (standing up for yourself and or living your truth)

8. You're trying to be relevant in other people's lives

9. You're caught up in feelings of guilt – let them go…

Now we see the importance of thinking of ourselves in terms of what we want to experience and why however we think of ourselves is our truth because as quantum physics says, "all times exist simultaneously in the now moment".

When we get emotional, where is the root of that? It's in the past. What does Christ consciousness mean? It means no past! We are all stuck in the past and our primary objective should be to deal with that. We cannot be free to time travel whilst we are stuck in it.

Living in the now is our natural timeless state. Part of the mind-control here is to get everyone conditioned to time, even though man-made time is just that. Time is really dimensional; it's a condition of consciousness and explains the different frequencies and dimensions.

We age by the clock because we are caught mentally in that condition and thus our minds are emotionally stuck in the past. Today and tomorrow are similar to yesterday because instead of using our minds creatively, we use them reactively (emotionally). We trigger our emotions everyday to make us feel alive; it's as simple as chatting to others, watching soapy dramas and reading novels.

You are a Timeless Being stuck in Time. Only you can free yourself. All of your emotional roots, trauma and weaknesses are in (coming from) your past. That's why you get huge 'releases' when you dig this stuff up and bring it to the surface.

Wisdom is key; it enables you to become the non-reactive observer, which is timeless ~ Gary Bate.

I only have beautiful experiences

The title of my book is one of my frequently used affirmations. It's worked particularly well whilst I've been walking our dogs. In fact, the altercations with other dogs have ceased and of course I have to give credit to creating my own reality.

I only have beautiful experiences and I live my life in harmony...

Working with consciousness and changing your mindset is a gradual refining and polishing process. I'm finding that I have to be consciously 'switched on' all of the time, as every thought counts in terms of what is flashing in front of my observer and creating my reality.

Don't worry if you're on an ugly train; just make sure you arrive at a beautiful destination. In other words, it's how you conclude your trains of thought that counts...

Everyday is an opportunity to re-define and polish yourself. It doesn't matter what happened yesterday, because you're now moving forward and you're not dragging any mules behind you.

Your new life starts now! Every one of you can do better. It's all attitude, so fix it and start living your life with an improved attitude. I know I'm making it sound simple but that's because it is!

It doesn't matter what other people do and say –

they're going to die! Let it go... It only matters what you say and do and how you treat other people. You are at the very core of everything that happens to you. You are the cause not the effect.

Everyone, including you, has acted in despicable ways at some time in their life. Get over it. You're no better than they are and they're no better than you are. Get your focus off other people. Your life is only really about YOU. Fix the cause...

'They' always divert your attention away from the culprits (themselves) and onto one of their created enemies. Putin is their ideal scapegoat. He's tucked away in the land of the bear where us commoners can't get to him. The irony is, he is one of them and so he is a culprit! Just like Gorbachev was, Putin is owned by the International Bankers – the same people who own just about everything else. He's happy to play the 'bad guy' for them.

Planet Earth is a conjob. The sooner you see it the sooner you can go into rehab.

The 'Firm' includes the Rothchilds and the head of the Rothchilds is the main entity. These people are psychicly connected to off-World entities who are controlling this planet via these people. The daily feed is what keeps everyone distracted away from this truth and onto the made-up enemy.

Divide the masses to control them has always worked and it continues to work indefinitely because people are buying the lie that their daily misery is down to one man in the 'enemy' country.

This energy crises has been deliberately created and all the World's leaders are in on it. You think it matters whether Truss or Sunak get's in? It doesn't matter! They're both owned by the Firm and they're both Zionists. The job of Truss or Sunak is to stick to the plan and gradually move the herd to a Conditional Universal Basic Income.

We are in this mess because we have been sporting a victim consciousness, which is the perfect yin yang balance for a small number of psychopathic tyrants to do whatever they like with us.

The way out is for everyone to finally put a foot down and say NO. A dystopian World is staring us all in the face. If we don't say NO now, we will suffer extreme hardship because their corporations control our lives and their progammable, digital currencies, will be in place by 2024.

It's super ok that you've had a long sleep whilst your attention has been distracted away from the truth and upon a fabricated illusion. Life is still life even when it's illusionary! But really, we're all at the 11th hour now and it's time for you to open your beautiful new eyes ~ Gary Bate.

Copyright Gary Bate September 2022

Afterword

This book is a combination of my own wisdom (that which I've experienced) and what I believe to be true (that which I have yet to experience).

The chapter on death is a good example. I have probably experienced it many times before, but the only memories I have, relate to my numerous out of body experiences. I obviously believe that my conclusions about death are accurate; but of course your experience of it may differ.

When you absorb the material contained herein, it will expand you and that's a good thing because that will invite new experiences, which will prove, one way or the other, what I've written. In this way you will gain in wisdom.

I believe that my work will take you deeper and in that way I have served you on a deeper level. I apologise for the lack of humour and for what will appear to be some condescending comments. There is no doubt in my mind, that at our deepest level, we are far superior to our human conditioning...

Please don't recommend this book because you think people will 'like it'; do so because it will serve them on their deepest level ~ Gary Bate.

Other Books by Gary Bate

We are here to know ourselves

The Question Is

Soul Completion

The Impeccable Journey

Pure Mind

Available via whatstress.com

Lightning Source UK Ltd.
Milton Keynes UK
UKHW020735220922
409267UK00010B/1004